Liverpool FC
The Greatest
GOALS

Zarif Rasul is a leading sports journalist based in Madrid, who writes for a number of publications around the world. During his time in England he wrote for virtually every English newspaper and appeared on Sky News and talkSPORT radio. Zarif is an ardent Reds supporter and cites Steven Gerrard (2) vs West Ham United in 2006 as his favourite Liverpool goal of all time.

First published by Carlton Books in 2015

Carlton Books
20 Mortimer Street
London W1T 3JW

A CIP catalogue for this book is available from the British Library.

ISBN 978-1-78097-664-8

10 9 8 7 6 5 4 3 2 1

Printed in Dubai

Following pages: *Liverpool's all-time leading goalscorer, Ian Rush, reels away in celebration after scoring the club's third goal in their 3-1 victory over Everton in the 1986 FA Cup Final.*

Liverpool FC
The Greatest
GOALS

ZARIF RASUL

CARLTON
BOOKS

CONTENTS

Right: *Spanish striker Fernando Torres regains his balance as he waits for his curled shot to bend its way beyond Chelsea goalkeeper Petr Cech and clinch a 2-0 league win for Liverpool in November 2010.*

INTRODUCTION

Liverpool Football Club has enjoyed a rich and successful history since it was formed by John Houlding on 15 March, 1892.

The 41 major trophies won during Liverpool FC's glorious existence have undoubtedly put the city on the global map and established the club as one of the world's elite.

And while the continuous flow of silverware has thrilled and delighted the supporters, it is the fabulous catalogue of goals, both at Anfield and away from home, which has really left an indelible mark on several generations of devoted fans.

Left: *Liverpool legend Kenny Dalglish celebrates scoring against Chelsea in 1986. The 1-0 victory secured Liverpool's 16th league title.*

Some of the world's finest football players have passed through the Anfield gates over the past 123 years, and many of them have elicited roars from the Kop or gasps of awe on the road after scoring in the famous red shirt.

No supporters who watched on in the 1970s will ever forget some of the strikes that secured the club's first European trophies, just as those of the younger generation will always remember impressive feats from their modern-day heroes.

The following collection of 50 sensational goals will certainly bring back wonderfully joyous memories or provoke interest and fascination among supporters of all ages.

Right: *Daniel Sturridge looks on as his sumptuous chip flies home against West Bromwich Albion in 2013.*

Following page: *Steven Gerrard scores the first of the come-back goals against AC Milan during the 2005 UEFA Champions League Final. Liverpool turned around a 3-0 deficit to triumph on penalties.*

LIVERPOOL FC: THE GREATEST GOALS

From booming headers, to intricate team moves, to sizzling 30-yard screamers, opposition teams have been devastated by an array of wonderful Liverpool strikes over the years.

Billy **LIDDELL**

DREAM LEAGUE DEBUT

Due to the outbreak of World War II, William Beveridge Liddell, better known as Billy, had to wait eight years to make his league debut for Liverpool. The day finally arrived in September 1946, and it couldn't have gone any better.

Billy Liddell, who was an accountant by trade, did not receive a single booking in his entire career.

The 7th of September 1946 is a momentous day in the history of Liverpool Football Club, as it witnessed the league debuts of not one, but two bona fide club legends – Billy Liddell and Bob Paisley. The former was at his mesmerising best on that late-summer afternoon, scoring twice as Liverpool raced into a 6-0 lead inside 50 minutes. Liddell, a powerful and skilful two-footed winger, needed less than two minutes to make his mark, demonstrating his superb technique to score direct from a corner-kick, which was won by his fellow league debutant. The Scot showcased his courage and combative nature after the break, embarking on a mazy dribble which took him past several opponents before bravely firing home. The league title would head to Anfield at the end of the season, with Liddell's attacking endeavours at the heart of their success.

" Liddell means so much to his side."

Ernest 'Bee' Edwards, *Liverpool Daily Post*

FIRST DIVISION | 7 September 1946

LIVERPOOL 7	Chelsea 4
Liddell 2, 50	*Goulden 55*
Jones 24, 30	*Argue 64*
W Fagan 44, 87	*Machin 70, 72*
Balmer 47	

Albert **STUBBINS**

THE GOAL IN THE SNOW

Albert Stubbins was greatly admired for his courage and commitment, thanks in no small part to an incredible act of bravery on a bitterly cold afternoon against Birmingham City.

The Anfield pitch was smothered in ice and snow, ravaged by the freezing winter, but that mattered not to Albert Stubbins as he lingered outside the box and awaited delivery of the ball from his team-mate Billy Liddell. Stubbins had already opened his account in the first half, only to see Frank Mitchell attain parity for Birmingham. Stubbins re-established the lead a minute later and, after Jack Balmer made it 3-1, he killed off Birmingham's hopes with one of the most famous goals in Anfield's long and rich history. Liddell drilled a venomous low free-kick into the area. Moments earlier, Stubbins had started to sprint forward, at full pelt. The striker timed his run to perfection, diving at full length to get his head on to the ball that had evaded everyone and redirect it into the net from close range. Stubbins, who had been less than a foot off the ground as he headed home, soldiered on with the bloodied knees he had sustained after crashing into the icy turf to score once again and complete his hat-trick.

" Both of my knees were lacerated and bleeding but it was certainly worth it."

Albert Stubbins

Albert Stubbins is the only footballer who appears on The Beatles' Sgt. Pepper's Lonely Hearts Club Band album cover artwork.

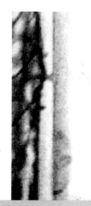

FA CUP | 1 March 1947

LIVERPOOL	**4**	1	Birmingham City
Stubbins 33, 57, 74			*Mitchell 56*
Balmer 64			

Roger HUNT

A FINE FINISH FOR THE SILVER SCREEN

Defending champions Liverpool started their season with a bang as goal machine Roger Hunt made television history.

Roger Hunt's 31 league goals had powered Liverpool to the 1963-64 league title and the England striker started the following campaign in a similar vein, striking early on in clinical fashion against Arsenal. Gordon Wallace won the ball in midfield and fed Peter Thompson on the left. The winger showcased great poise and trickery, drawing one tackle and skipping past it with consummate ease before checking his run and cutting back on to his right foot as another opponent approached. Thompson's ball to the far side of the box was high but Ian Callaghan managed to chest it down, adroitly, before dinking it back to Hunt on the penalty spot. Hunt was facing away from goal, toward the right corner flag, but that didn't matter, as he adjusted his body perfectly to hook a looping volley just under the crossbar and into the top left-hand corner. It was the first goal ever to be broadcast on the BBC's Match of the Day programme, as well as the strike that set Liverpool on their way to an opening-day win.

FIRST DIVISION | 22 August 1964

LIVERPOOL	**3**	2	Arsenal
Hunt 11			Strong 64
Wallace 49, 87			Baker 65

" Wallace...Thompson...is it too high for Callaghan? No. Hunt...it's a goal!"

Kenneth Wolstenholme's match commentary

Ian **ST JOHN**

THIRD TIME LUCKY

Liverpool's two previous FA Cup Final appearances, in 1914 and 1950, ended with the heartbreak of defeat. They didn't need divine intervention to end that run in 1965, but the presence of a 'Saint' certainly proved decisive in the second half of extra-time.

Ian St John was signed for a then club-record fee of £37,500 from Motherwell in 1961.

The tension was starting to grow at Wembley once again, although Liverpool were coping better than their opponents with the mounting fatigue. With nine minutes left on the clock, Ian Callaghan surged down the right-hand side of the box, gliding effortlessly across the turf as if it was the first minute, not the 111th. As he approached the byline, he glanced up and cut the ball back across the face of goal. Goalkeeper Gary Sprake came out from his near post to thwart the cross but the ball evaded his grasp. Ian St John, stationed in the centre of the six-yard box, flung his head at the ball. Defender Paul Reaney, who was covering on the goal-line, could do nothing as the ball dropped over the white line, beyond the reach of his left foot, and rolled into the back of the net. The FA Cup was Liverpool's at long last.

" I moved into position for a short [cross] and the hunch paid off – the ball dropped just right."

Ian St John

FA CUP FINAL | 1 May 1965

LIVERPOOL	**2**	1	Leeds United
Hunt 93			*Bremner 102*
St John 111			

Kevin KEEGAN

MIGHTY MOUSE'S GOALS SEAL UEFA CUP

Kevin Keegan scored 100 goals in 323 appearances for Liverpool.

Kevin Keegan scored numerous goals in the 1972–73 season, but none were as important as the brace that ultimately secured the club's first European trophy.

The bog-like conditions at a sodden Anfield did not hamper the hosts, who raced into a two-goal lead. Chris Lawler, who was in acres of space on the right, launched the ball crossfield into the box toward Toshack, who towered above his marker to nod the ball into Keegan's path. Keegan, who was parallel to the ground as he met the ball, dived across the muddy turf to send a firm header into the left-hand corner. Keegan could've doubled his tally shortly afterwards, but his penalty was turned around the post by Wolfgang Kleff. Far from being disheartened by his miss, Keegan was in the thick of it again in the 33rd minute when he latched on to another Toshack knockdown and instinctively finished from 10 yards out. Gladbach's task became even more difficult when Larry Lloyd made it 3-0 in the second half, while Ray Clemence produced a superb save to deny Jupp Heynckes from the penalty spot and maintain his clean sheet. Gladbach won 2–0 in the return leg but it was not enough to prevent Liverpool from etching their name on to the UEFA Cup.

" Lawler…Toshack…Keegan… one-nil!"

David Coleman's match commentary

UEFA CUP FINAL FIRST LEG	10 May 1973		
LIVERPOOL	**3**	0	Borussia Mönchengladbach
Keegan 21, 33			
Lloyd 62			

Kevin KEEGAN

THE PERFECT PAIR

Kevin Keegan and John Toshack dovetailed beautifully to form one of English football's classic strike partnerships. They exhibited their telepathic understanding to devastating effect to down Leicester.

A scoreless FA Cup semi-final replay at Villa Park sparked into life after half-time, with a goal for each side within three minutes of the restart. Kevin Keegan had been desperately unlucky not to get himself on the scoresheet during the first match, but he earned a reward for his persistent endeavour when he re-established Liverpool's advantage in the 62nd minute. The move started when his strike partner, John Toshack, dropped deep to tend to a loose ball. Clocking Keegan's run in behind, the giant Welshman looped a high ball through to his diminutive colleague. Keegan nipped in between Leicester's centre-backs and, with Peter Shilton six yards off his line, confidently volleyed a first-time effort over the goalkeeper and into the back of the net. Toshack struck late on to secure Liverpool's place in the Final at Wembley, where they would swat aside Newcastle United to lift their second FA Cup.

FA CUP | 3 April 1974

LIVERPOOL	3	1	Leicester City
Hall 46			Glover 48
Keegan 62			
Toshack 86			

" Toshack…that's for Keegan… what a goal! What can you say about Kevin Keegan?"

David Coleman's match commentary

David **FAIRCLOUGH**

DERBY DAY DRAMA

A run of three successive league wins had revived Liverpool's title challenge, but that momentum was set to grind to a halt as Everton frustrated Bob Paisley's men at Anfield.

A fiercely fought Merseyside derby looked as though it was going to end in a stalemate until substitute David Fairclough enthralled Anfield with a cunning combination of persistence and opportunism two minutes from time. The visitors' Martin Dobson, who was five yards adrift of the halfway line, launched his throw-in at Roger Kenyon, who tried to play it back to him. However, Kenyon's pass was poor and was intercepted by Fairclough, who admirably showed great strength to hold off Dobson. Motoring on, Fairclough evaded Kenyon's attempt to recover the ball with a lunging tackle and headed inward. Dave Jones, who was next in line to try to dispossess Fairclough, could only watch on as the nimble 19-year-old switched the ball to his right foot and advanced forward through the corner of the area. As the angle narrowed, Fairclough surprised goalkeeper Dai Davies by drilling a fierce low effort in at the near post. Fairclough had single-handedly won the game for Liverpool and renewed the club's title charge.

David Fairclough scored against 31 different teams during his time at Liverpool.

" ... to score a winner and be remembered for it is something I'll have all my life." **David Fairclough**

FIRST DIVISION	3 April 1976		
LIVERPOOL	**1**	0	Everton
Fairclough 88			

David FAIRCLOUGH

SUPERSUB SLAYS SAINT-ETIENNE

One goal was all Liverpool needed to progress to the last four of the European Cup. Bob Paisley rolled the dice and introduced David Fairclough off the bench; the manager was rewarded handsomely.

Time was running out for Liverpool, but the hope in the supporters' hearts had not yet faded. With six minutes left on the clock, Ray Kennedy, who was five yards inside his own half, volleyed the ball high into the Merseyside night, beyond the visitors' defence at the other end of the field. The ball bounced once as Fairclough, who had accelerated into the space and trapped the ball, held off the challenge of Christian Lopez and advanced toward the area. As he entered the box, the lithe flame-haired forward coolly steadied himself, while Anfield held its breath. Goalkeeper Ivan Curkovic came off his line but it was no use, as Fairclough, with ice in his veins, slid the ball toward the near post, into the back of the net. The 24,000 assembled on the Kop surged forward like never before, as Anfield shook to its foundations.

> " *The amazing thing is, it seemed so quiet as I homed in on the target but when the ball hit the back of the net the noise was just unbelievable.*"
>
> **David Fairclough**

EUROPEAN CUP | 16 March 1977

LIVERPOOL	**3**	1	Saint-Etienne
Keegan 2			*Bathenay 51*
Kennedy 59			
Fairclough 84			

Jimmy CASE

TURN AND VOLLEY

Liverpool's hopes of securing English football's first domestic and European treble were dashed by their fiercest rivals, but the travelling Kopites at Wembley were at least left with the memory of a sumptuous Jimmy Case strike.

Five manic minutes ultimately decided the winners of the 96th FA Cup Final, with Jimmy Case's sublime equaliser for Liverpool sandwiched by Stuart Pearson's opener and Jimmy Greenhoff's winner. Stunned by Pearson's breakthrough, Liverpool poured forward and levelled just one minute later. Joey Jones, who was inside the United half on the left, cut on to his right foot and drifted a long ball forward toward the box. Case, who was facing away from goal, cushioned the ball down on his right thigh with his first touch before nudging it to his left, to the edge of the box, with his second. In one fell swoop, the young midfielder swivelled on a sixpence and, with the ball inches off the ground, hooked a marvellous right-footed shot beyond Alex Stepney into the top right-hand corner. It was some way for the 23-year-old to mark his maiden Wembley appearance.

Midfield powerhouse Jimmy Case scored 23 times in 186 appearances for Liverpool.

"Jones…Case…good turn…oh yes! A brilliant goal by Jimmy Case!"

John Motson's match commentary

FA CUP FINAL	21 May 1977		
LIVERPOOL	1	2	Manchester United
Case 52			*J Pearson 51*
			Greenhoff 55

Tommy SMITH

ANFIELD IRON FLATTENS GLADBACH

Liverpool, in their fourth European Cup campaign, had finally reached the competition's showpiece event; they were just 90 minutes away from bringing 'Big Ears' back to Merseyside.

The 24,000 travelling Kopites at Rome's Olympic Stadium were thrilled after Terry McDermott finished neatly from inside the box to put Liverpool in front, but Allan Simonsen got Gladbach back on track with a rifled effort six minutes after half-time. The match was on a knife-edge when Hans Klinkhammer conceded a corner on the left in the 63rd minute. Steve Heighway, on set-piece duty, commenced his run-up from the running track that circled the pitch. Meanwhile, Tommy Smith had taken the first few steps of his diagonal dash toward the near post. Heighway flighted his corner with pace and whip and Smith, who had already advanced forward 10 yards, leaped powerfully to meet the ball with a firm header which soared into the roof of the net. Lifelong Red Smith, on his 600th appearance, had turned the tide in Liverpool's favour, while Phil Neal's late penalty secured the result and the first of the club's five European Cups.

Tommy Smith, who made 638 appearances for Liverpool, scored 48 goals for the club.

" It was possibly the most important European touch in Liverpool's history."

Tommy Smith

EUROPEAN CUP FINAL	25 May 1977		
LIVERPOOL	**3**	1	Borussia
McDermott 27			Mönchengladbach
Smith 64			*Simonsen 51*
Neal 82			

Kenny **DALGLISH**

KING KENNY'S CORONATION

Liverpool splashed out a British transfer record fee to bring in Kenny Dalglish as a replacement for Kevin Keegan in the summer of 1977, and they didn't have to wait long for a return on their investment.

A combination of errant finishing and Bruges' defensive approach kept the game scoreless until shortly after the hour mark. A touch of finesse was needed, and it was provided by the man who had cost £440,000 the year before. Kenny Dalglish hooked in a high cross from the right, but Daniël de Cubber headed it away. Graeme Souness used two touches to control the ball, waited, and as the Bruges defensive line moved forward as one, threaded a gorgeously weighted ball through to Dalglish. With the offside trap beaten, Dalglish, who was advancing toward the right side of the six-yard box, coolly clipped the ball over Birger Jensen, using his right foot like a pitching wedge, as the goalkeeper rushed out to narrow the angle. Realising the magnitude of what he'd done, Dalglish jubilantly skipped over the advertising hoardings to celebrate in front of the Liverpool fans, before turning round to his team-mates who had rushed forward to embrace him. 'Big Ears' was staying at Anfield.

> " *Souness played the ball through from the edge of the box ... and I just clipped it over the keeper and into the goal.*"
>
> **Kenny Dalglish**

EUROPEAN CUP FINAL | 10 May 1978

LIVERPOOL	**1**	0 FC Bruges
Dalglish 65		

Kenny Dalglish's clipped effort evades the outstretched leg of FC Bruges goalkeeper Birger Jensen and heads toward the far corner of the net. The Scotsman's strike earned Liverpool their second consecutive European Cup.

Terry McDERMOTT

SEVENTH HEAVEN

Spurs had succumbed to Liverpool's verve and vibrancy, conceding six times in 64 minutes, but it was the seventh strike which ended up in the back of Barry Daines' net that really defied superlatives.

It was a ball from goalkeeper Ray Clemence to Ray Kennedy that initiated one of the greatest box-to-box goals of all time. From there Kennedy fed Dalglish, who played the ball forward to David Johnson. Situated on the halfway line, the substitute sprayed the ball into the path of Steve Heighway, who was galloping down the left wing. Heighway, at full speed, angled a glorious left-footed cross into the box. The ball hung in the air for the requisite amount of time before McDermott, who had been at the edge of his own area less than ten seconds earlier, arrived at the right time to hurl himself forward at breakneck speed and power home a bullet header from just outside the six-yard box. It was counter-attacking football at its most clinical and most scintillating, and it set the tone for what was to follow over the coming months as Liverpool sauntered toward their 11th league title.

"That must be the best goal Anfield has ever seen."

Bob Paisley

Terry McDermott scored 81 times in 329 outings for Liverpool.

FIRST DIVISION | 2 September 1978

LIVERPOOL   7   0 Tottenham Hotspur
Dalglish 8, 20
R Kennedy 28
Johnson 48, 58
Neal 64, McDermott 76

Terry McDERMOTT

UP AND AWAY

Terry McDermott scored 16 goals in the 1979–80 season; none were as impressive as the one he netted in north London to send Liverpool into the last four of the FA Cup.

With the likes of Glenn Hoddle, Ricky Villa and Ossie Ardiles lining up for the hosts, and aesthetes such as Kenny Dalglish and Alan Hansen on the opposing side, it's safe to say there was no shortage of flair and technical ability when Spurs and Liverpool battled for a place in the FA Cup semi-finals. Liverpool were cruising at the top of the league table at the time, 18 points above 15th-placed Spurs, and they edged the encounter at White Hart Lane thanks to Terry McDermott's wonderful moment of improvised brilliance, which ended up winning the BBC's goal of the season. Ardiles, pegged back into the left-back position in his own half under pressure from Jimmy Case, carelessly ceded the ball to McDermott, 22 yards out on the right-hand side. The midfielder, with no white shirts near him, nonchalantly rolled the ball up to tee himself up and struck an exquisite volley, which formed a perfect arc as it soared through the air before nestling in the top left-hand corner.

Terry McDermott became the first player to win the FWA Footballer of the Year and PFA Player of the Year awards in the same season when he picked up both gongs in 1980.

" I caught my shot just right."

Terry McDermott

FA CUP | 8 March 1980

Tottenham Hotspur   0   **1 LIVERPOOL**
                                          McDermott 38

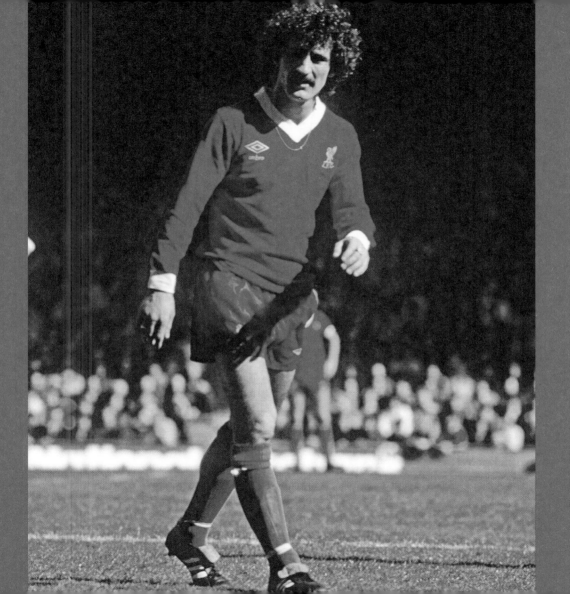

Graeme **SOUNESS**

THE SOUNESS SHOW

The road to Paris, the venue for the 1981 European Cup Final, had been a smooth one for Liverpool, who saw off CSKA Sofia with the aid of a Graeme Souness masterclass.

Graeme Souness' one-man tour de force on an early spring evening in 1981, when he book-ended a Liverpool rout as well as scoring their third, all but secured the Reds' berth in the last four of the European Cup. Having broken the deadlock in the 16th minute, Souness made it 3-0 with a trademark thunderbolt. Kenny Dalglish led a string of CSKA Sofia players on a merry dance before squaring into space just outside the 'D'. Souness arrived, on cue, and after checking his run ever so slightly, placed the ball into the top left-hand corner with ease. He completed CSKA's misery with ten minutes remaining. Phil Neal lofted the ball toward the right wing, where Steve Heighway let the ball advance toward the goal-line before pulling it back into the box. Ray Kennedy lunged across the floor and headed it back toward the edge of the box. Souness arrived at the perfect moment and thumped a fizzing half-volley into the right-hand corner at the Kop end from 20 yards out.

Graeme Souness won trophies for Liverpool as both player and manager.

" Souness…oh I say! What a way to complete a hat-trick! He never saw it."

Barry Davies's match commentary

EUROPEAN CUP | 4 March 1981

LIVERPOOL	**5**	1	CSKA Sofia
Souness 16, 51, 80			*Ionchev 57*
Lee 45			
McDermott 62			

Alan KENNEDY

*Remarkably, Alan
Kennedy scored
the winning goal in
two European Cup
Finals – he also
netted the decisive
spot-kick in the
penalty shootout
win against Roma
in 1984.*

BARNEY'S BURST

**Liverpool's quest for a third European Cup in five years led
them to the Final in Paris, where they were pitted against
genuine continental aristocrats, six-time winners Real Madrid.**

Paris' Parc des Princes was a suitably regal setting for the meeting
of two clubs with a combined total of eight European Cups between
them. Given their continental experience, a close affair ensued, with
nothing to separate them until the 81st minute, when Alan Kennedy's
burst from the back culminated in the only goal of the game. Ray
Kennedy took a long throw-in from the left-hand touchline and his
namesake, up in nosebleed territory, chested it down a yard outside
the box. With unstoppable momentum gathering, the left-back surged
into the area. García Cortés stuck a leg out in an attempt to thwart
his movement forward, but it was all in vain. Bearing down on the
advancing goalkeeper Agustín, Kennedy fired a diagonal shot of pure
power toward the near post. His arms were already aloft in celebration
by the time the ball crashed against the net on the far side. 'Barney,
Barney' cried the travelling Reds, as the 12,000 supporters from the
Spanish capital fell silent.

EUROPEAN CUP FINAL | 27 May 1981

LIVERPOOL   **1**   0   Real Madrid
A Kennedy 81

*" It was just one of those where you put your
foot through it and hope for the best."*

Alan Kennedy

Real Madrid goalkeeper Agustín can do nothing to keep out Alan Kennedy's fierce near-post strike, which propels Liverpool to their third European Cup win in five years.

Ian **RUSH**

RUSHIE'S EYE FOR GOAL

Liverpool and Ipswich were just two of the clubs engaged in a nine-way battle for the title; the Reds underlined their credentials by mauling the Tractor Boys at Anfield.

Ipswich Town held a two-point advantage over Liverpool but saw that wiped out as the rampant Reds ran riot in the second of the two sides' three meetings inside the space of a week. Liverpool, who had won at Portman Road in the first leg of the League Cup semi-final four days before, came flying out of the blocks, striking twice inside the opening 20 minutes. Ian Rush, still only 20, was enjoying a wonderful first full season at Liverpool, with 18 goals in his previous 23 outings, and he showcased his burgeoning predatory instinct in the 17th minute. Ronnie Whelan steamed forward from the middle of the park and laid the ball off to Kenny Dalglish before continuing his run into the box. The Scot's return ball was diverted into the path of Rush, who took two steps toward the ball before caressing it, with power and curl, into the bottom right-hand corner.

Ian Rush scored 30 or more goals in a season on five separate occasions during his time at Liverpool.

"Ian Rush sensed an opening and blazed a way past Cooper."

Martin Tyler's match commentary

FIRST DIVISION | 6 February 1982

LIVERPOOL   **4**   0   Ipswich Town
McDermott 14
Rush 17
Dalglish 44
Whelan 57

Ronnie WHELAN

WHELAN SENDS PAISLEY OFF IN STYLE

Ronnie Whelan had made his mark in the League Cup with two goals in the 1982 Final; he was at it again the following year to mark Bob Paisley's last visit to Wembley with a win.

Liverpool and the League Cup trophy were seemingly inseparable in the early part of the 1980s, and it was the competition in which Ronnie Whelan really began to establish himself as an Anfield hero. Having struck a brace to vanquish Tottenham under the famous Twin Towers 12 months previously, Whelan devastated Manchester United with a glorious extra-time winner after Alan Kennedy had cancelled out Norman Whiteside's strike to force extra-time. Eight minutes into extra-time, Kennedy, making one of his trademark buccaneering runs from the back, initiated a one-two with Whelan, who was positioned on the left-hand corner of the United box. The Irishman tried to return the ball, but his pass was cut out. As the ball returned to him, Whelan took one step, adjusted his body perfectly, and bent the ball, with judicious precision, into the top right-hand corner, despite goalkeeper Gary Bailey's best efforts to get to the ball.

Both Ronnie Whelan and his father, also named Ronnie, appeared for the Republic of Ireland at senior international level.

" Kennedy…Whelan…and again, Whelan's curled it!"

John Motson's match commentary

LEAGUE CUP FINAL	26 March 1983	
LIVERPOOL	**2**	1 Manchester United
A Kennedy 75		*Whiteside 12*
Whelan 98		

Graeme SOUNESS

SOUNESS SEALS QUARTET

One hundred and twenty minutes at Wembley had failed to separate the two Merseyside rivals; something truly special was needed at Maine Road to decide the destination of the League Cup trophy.

Liverpool had triumphed in the League Cup during each of the previous three seasons and some typically decisive play from inspirational captain Graeme Souness ensured the trophy remained in the Reds' grip for a further year. Phil Neal, who had received the ball from Kenny Dalglish, passed forward to Graeme Souness, who appeared to be in an unthreatening position, with his back to goal, 30 yards away from goalkeeper Neville Southall. But then the Scot flicked the ball up, with the spin deceiving his marker. As he turned, Souness threw forward his left foot with venom and connected with a dipping volley, which bounced just before the goal and continued its journey past Southall before hitting the net. Manager Joe Fagan, in his first year in charge after succeeding the club's most successful manager Bob Paisley, had his first piece of silverware. Two more, the league title and the European Cup, would follow before the season was out.

" *[I] flashed a leg at it and it just dipped in front of Everton keeper Neville Southall before going in.*"

Graeme Souness

LEAGUE CUP FINAL | 28 March 1984

LIVERPOOL   **1**   0   Everton
Souness 21

Jan **MOLBY**

'LOST' GOAL SECURES THE CUP

On a cold night in November 1985, Jan Molby tore right through the heart of Manchester United to provide Anfield with a very special goal.

A TV rights dispute at the start of the 1985–86 season meant that Liverpool's League Cup clash with Manchester United was not broadcast. It also robbed the wider world of one of the finest individual strikes Anfield has ever seen, a goal that, until footage eventually emerged 24 years later, was spoken of in hushed tones among the 41,291 who were in attendance on the 26th of November 1985. Liverpool had trailed Manchester United thanks to Paul McGrath's early opener, but Jan Molby attained parity in quite sensational circumstances. Ten yards inside his own half, the Dane robbed Norman Whiteside of the ball by the left touchline. From there, he embarked on a mesmerisingly direct run toward the United box, gliding across the Anfield turf like a gazelle on the Serengeti. Clayton Blackmore made an attempt to dispossess him but Molby passed him as if he wasn't there. Now two yards shy of the area, Molby unleashed a rising cannon of a shot which went past goalkeeper Gary Bailey in the blink of an eye.

> *"Gary Bailey, the United keeper, still insists it was the hardest shot he had ever faced."*
>
> *Jan Molby*

Jan Molby was deadly from the penalty spot, scoring 42 of 45 spot-kicks during his time at Liverpool.

LEAGUE CUP	26 November 1985		
LIVERPOOL		**2**	1 Manchester United
Molby 57, 58			*McGrath 7*

Kenny **DALGLISH**

THE KING DELIVERS SWEET TITLE 16

Liverpool were three points away from regaining the league title in player-manager Kenny Dalglish's first season in the dug-out; there was only ever one man who was going to push them over the finishing line.

A long throw came into the Chelsea box, but it was only partially cleared out to Ronnie Whelan, 35 yards from goal. The Irishman trapped the ball and attempted a wild shot, which ricocheted off his marker and ended up in the air. With his eyes firmly fixed on the ball, Whelan headed to Gary Beglin, who had his back to goal. The young defender, having glanced over his shoulder moments earlier, volleyed a superb looping pass through to Dalglish, who was, inexplicably, unmarked inside the box. The player-manager tamed the ball, killing its momentum with the upper-right part of his chest, before taking a further step forward and volleying past Tony Godden into the far right-hand corner from eight yards out. Liverpool were on course to record their first league win at Chelsea in over 12 years, while the title was set to head back to Anfield at the first time of asking for Dalglish.

Kenny Dalglish is one of only four men who have guided two different top-flight clubs to the league title as a manager.

" And Dalglish is in here…yes! "

John Motson's match commentary

FIRST DIVISION | 3 May 1986

Chelsea	0	**1 LIVERPOOL**
		Dalglish 23

Ian **RUSH**

Ian Rush has
scored more FA
Cup Final goals
(five) than any
other player in
the competition's
long history.

DOUBLE DELIGHT

Since the turn of the 20th century, only two clubs had won the First Division league title and the FA Cup in the same season; Liverpool were about to become the third.

With two of the nation's most lethal marksmen, Ian Rush and Gary Lineker, on show, an open FA Cup Final was expected, and so it proved to be. Lineker's rebound effort shortly before the half-hour mark made it 1-0, but Rush responded 30 minutes later, rounding Neville Southall before rolling the ball into the empty net. Six minutes later, Craig Johnston arrived unmarked at the back post to turn the match on its head. And as Everton went in search of an equaliser, Liverpool caught them cold to put the game beyond their reach. A slick blur of red shirts moved the ball forward from inside their own half to the edge of the opposition box, where Ronnie Whelan checked his run. As Kenny Dalglish overlapped on the left, Whelan instead lofted the ball to the edge of the six-yard box on the far side, where Rush met the cross before firing low and hard into the opposite corner, smashing a camera in the process. Liverpool had finally secured their first Double, while Dalglish had become the first player-manager to win the FA Cup.

FA CUP FINAL | 10 May 1986

LIVERPOOL   **3**   1   Everton
Rush 57, 84   *Lineker 27*
Johnston 63

*" The man never fails from
that sort of position."*

Brian Moore's match commentary

Steve **NICOL**

CHICO GETS REDS OFF TO A FLYER

All eyes were on Liverpool's exciting new signings Peter Beardsley and John Barnes, but the Reds' opening-day winner at Highbury came from an unlikely source.

A season's-best crowd of 54,703 were packed into Highbury on a scorching afternoon, and the majority were left bitterly disappointed when Steve Nicol snatched a dramatic late winner for the visiting side. Debutant John Barnes swung in a free-kick from the left, only to find the head of Tony Adams. However, the Arsenal defender's clearance only went as far as the edge of the box, where Nicol summoned incredible strength in his neck muscles to re-divert the ball over those assembled inside the box and goalkeeper John Lukic with a fabulous looping header. The goal ended up being the catalyst for a tremendous run, as Liverpool then went seven months and 28 league matches without defeat on the way to regaining the title.

The versatile Steve Nicol played in six different positions in the 1988–89 season as he won the FWA Footballer of the Year award.

" Barnes' free-kick came in…it was half-cleared by Arsenal straight to Nicol… and he returned it with full value beyond Lukic into the back of the net."

Brian Moore's match commentary

FIRST DIVISION	15 August 1987		
Arsenal		1	**2 LIVERPOOL**
Davis 17			*Aldridge 9*
			Nicol 88

John **BARNES**

DIGGER DESTROYS THE RANGERS

Kenny Dalglish's new-look side were characterised by exciting attacking endeavour and fluidity; no man symbolised this new approach more than the electrifying John Barnes.

In the summer of 1987, Liverpool supporters had reason to be glum – Ian Rush had left for Juventus, while the club had endured a rare trophyless season. However, good times were on the way as manager Kenny Dalglish's remodelled attack, which was conducted by new arrival John Barnes, carried the club back to glory with some of the finest performances English football has ever seen. QPR came to Anfield as potential title challengers in the autumn of 1987 but left with their ambitions lowered after being blitzed by Barnes and his cohorts. The Jamaica-born winger had a hand in all four of Liverpool's goals, but it was his second strike, the Reds' fourth of the match, which best epitomised his swashbuckling, snake-hipped style. After winning the ball from Kevin Brock on the halfway line, Barnes stormed forward like a freight train toward the QPR box and sashayed his way past three hapless defenders before placing the ball, low and precise, beyond David Seaman with his right foot.

John Barnes' performances in the 1987–88 season earned him the prestigious PFA Player of the Year and FWA Footballer of the Year awards.

"Barnes has so much skill and he livens up the game – he scored two great goals."

Ian Rush

FIRST DIVISION	17 October 1987		
LIVERPOOL	**4**	0	Queens Park Rangers
Johnston 41			
Aldridge 65			
Barnes 79, 85			

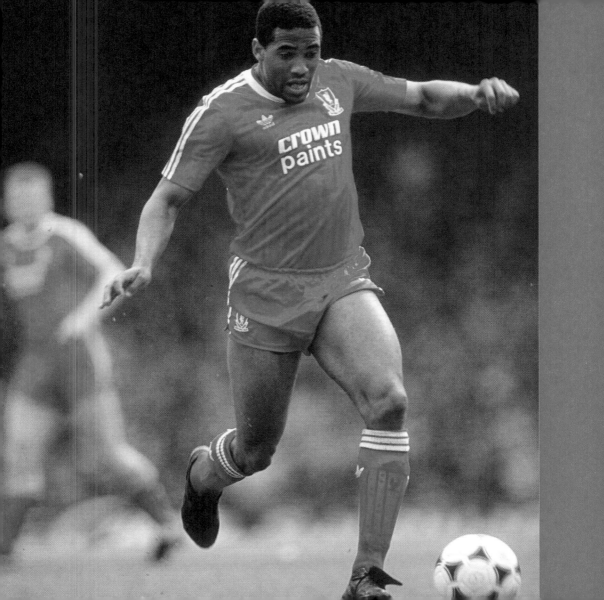

John **ALDRIDGE**

ALDO SENDS THE REDS TO WEMBLEY

John Aldridge was enjoying a sensational first full season at Anfield; his 24th and 25th goals of the campaign booked the Reds' place in the FA Cup Final.

Any doubts Liverpool fans may have had about the side's attacking thrust after the sale of Ian Rush the previous summer were quickly dispelled by the prolific form of John Aldridge, who went into the FA Cup semi-final against Nottingham Forest with 23 goals to his name. The Scouse striker's movement and finishing ability were eerily reminiscent of the departed Welshman, but he was also lethal from the spot, as he showed when he scored his 11th penalty of the season to put Liverpool in front at Hillsborough. He then went on to notch the eventual winner, shortly after the break, putting the finishing touch on a typically incisive counter-attacking move. John Barnes and Peter Beardsley showed an almost telepathic understanding of each other's movements as they exchanged a sequence of passes before the former curled a delicious ball across the face of goal from the left. Aldridge was in the right place at the right time, sliding in to volley home and send the travelling Reds into delirium.

" Barnes…Aldridge is there… Aldridge! Liverpool come out of defence and snatch a vital goal."

John Motson's match commentary

John Aldridge became Real Sociedad's first non-Basque signing of the modern era when he moved to the club from Liverpool in 1989.

FA CUP | 9 April 1988		
LIVERPOOL	**2**	1 Nottingham Forest
Aldridge 14, 51		*Clough 67*

Ian **RUSH**

With 346 goals, Ian Rush is Liverpool's all-time record goalscorer.

RUSH HAUNTS THE TOFFEES...AGAIN

The third all-Merseyside major cup final was finely poised until Ian Rush reprised his favourite role as Everton's tormentor-in-chief.

Kenny Dalglish's decision to take off goalscorer John Aldridge was a bold one, but the Liverpool manager knew what he was doing when he introduced Ian Rush into the fray in the 72nd minute of the FA Cup Final. After Stuart McCall's late equaliser forced extra-time, Rush restored the Reds' advantage with a neat swivel and finish before the Everton midfielder pegged them back once again. As the searing Wembley sun beat down on the 22 tired players, Rush kept his cool to turn the tide back in Liverpool's favour once and for all. With 17 minutes of extra-time remaining, John Barnes flighted an inch-perfect cross from the left toward the Welsh poacher, who got in between Everton's centre-backs and stooped to divert the ball, with his head, beyond Neville Southall from eight yards out. The goal was Rush's 21st against Everton – a new Merseyside derby record – but more importantly, it helped ensure a fitting way for Liverpool to honour the 95 supporters who had tragically died at Hillsborough only five weeks earlier.

> " *Beautiful ball by Barnes...deftest of headers by Rush ... steered it wide of Southall.*"
>
> **John Motson's match commentary**

FA CUP FINAL | 20 May 1989

LIVERPOOL	**3**	2 Everton
Aldridge 4		*McCall 89, 102*
Rush 94, 103		

Peter **BEARDSLEY**

BEARDSLEY DAZZLES

A breathless eight-goal derby proved to be the cue for King Kenny to depart his throne after 14 years, with Peter Beardsley's second-half stunner the pick of the action at Goodison Park.

Following a dour 0-0 draw at Anfield, Liverpool and Everton reconvened on the other side of Stanley Park three days later and produced one of the greatest FA Cup ties in the history of the world's oldest club competition. And at the heart of the proceedings lay Peter Beardsley, who twice gave the Reds the lead. The Geordie schemer's second was arguably the finest strike of the 59 he managed in 175 appearances for Liverpool. Picking up the ball 35 yards from goal, Beardsley, with his trademark dribbling style, weaved his way to the edge of the box before slamming an unstoppable left-footed drive past Neville Southall and into the far corner. A goal good enough to win any game, it put Liverpool 2-1 up, but it was soon cancelled out by Graeme Sharp's second of the night. Four more goals followed, including two in extra-time, to force a second replay, but by that point Liverpool had lost manager Kenny Dalglish, who resigned two days after the 4-4 thriller to leave Anfield in a state of shock.

Peter Beardsley scored the goal that clinched Liverpool's 17th league title in 1987–88 with the winner in a 1-0 victory over Tottenham.

"Beardsley…Barnes is free…oh my!"

Martin Tyler's match commentary

FA CUP | 20 February 1991

Everton	4	**4 LIVERPOOL**
Sharp 48, 73		*Beardsley 37, 71*
Cottee 89, 113		*Rush 77*
		Barnes 103

Robbie **FOWLER**

TOXTETH TERROR ON TARGET

Eric Cantona was the focus of attention on his return to the 'Theatre of Dreams', but the enigmatic Frenchman was upstaged by the bleached-blond tyro lining up for the away team.

Less than 120 seconds after kick-off, Eric Cantona centred for Nicky Butt to break the deadlock. As the majority of the Old Trafford crowd rejoiced in the return of their 'King', the small band of visiting supporters were about to bow down to 'God'. Shortly after the half-hour mark, Robbie Fowler latched on to a pass from Jamie Redknapp on the left-hand side. Using his first touch to carry the ball into the area, the young striker then despatched an explosive angled rocket which whizzed past the imposing Peter Schmeichel at his near post. The sheer force of Fowler's strike, his seventh of the season, nearly took the TV camera behind the goal off its hinges. He was at it again after the break, muscling Gary Neville aside to chip exquisitely over Schmeichel, but Cantona ensured parity with a penalty 19 minutes from time. Despite that, the afternoon belonged to Liverpool's prodigious No.23.

PREMIER LEAGUE | 1 October 1995

Manchester United 2 **2 LIVERPOOL**
Butt 2   *Fowler 33, 52*
Cantona 71

" Fowler's finishing was fantastic. The first one was good, but the second was absolutely first-class."

Sir Alex Ferguson

A jubilant Robbie Fowler rushes to embrace team-mate Jason McAteer after making it 1-1 against Manchester United at Old Trafford. The fresh-faced forward doubled his tally for the afternoon after the break.

Robbie **FOWLER**

THE MARK OF A GENIUS

Liverpool took Aston Villa apart with a blistering early onslaught at Anfield, with one man almost entirely responsible for the Midlanders' demise.

Robbie Fowler was on course to win his second consecutive PFA Young Player of the Year award and performances like his at Anfield on 3 May 1996 indicated why. Steve McManaman's volleyed opener in the second minute put the finishing touch on a well-worked move, but what followed three minutes later was born entirely of individual genius. McManaman, in the middle of the park, decided to feed Fowler, who had his back to goal, 35 yards out. Aware of Steve Staunton's presence behind him, Fowler tricked the former Liverpool defender with a Cruyff-like turn, completely taking him out of the game, and motored forward. With space opening up in front of him, Fowler picked out the far corner of Mark Bosnich's net with a venomous rising drive, before scampering off to celebrate with his adoring fans in the front row of the Kop. Three minutes later he had a second, taking his tally for the season to 29 goals.

Robbie Fowler scored more goals against Aston Villa (14) than he did against any other club over the course of his two spells at Liverpool.

> *" That's all about individual brilliance and confidence in a young man."*
>
> **Andy Gray's match commentary**

PREMIER LEAGUE | 3 March 1996

LIVERPOOL   **3**   0   Aston Villa
McManaman 2
Fowler 5, 8

Stan **COLLYMORE**

STAN SETTLES SEVEN-GOAL THRILLER

Stan Collymore became Britain's most expensive footballer when he joined Liverpool for £8.5m in 1995.

Over the course of 89 fast and furious minutes of frantic first-rate football, Anfield had witnessed six goals, with the lead changing hands on three occasions. Unfortunately for Newcastle, there was a sting left in the tail.

Liverpool's two most experienced campaigners, Ian Rush and John Barnes, took up one last charge for Roy Evans' side, neatly weaving their way into the Newcastle box with a rapid succession of short passes before finding themselves stuck in traffic. While all around him were losing their heads, Barnes had the presence of mind to pause to pick out the advancing Collymore on the left-hand side of the box. Collymore took one touch, got the ball out of his feet, and then lashed home at the near post, leaving goalkeeper Pavel Srníček with no chance. The striker jubilantly ran away up the touchline as former Kop idol Kevin Keegan slumped on the Anfield advertising hoardings, aware that his Newcastle side's title challenge was as good as over. Those in attendance at Anfield gasped for breath, having witnessed one of the greatest matches in Premier League history.

" Barnes…Rush…Barnes…still John Barnes…Collymore closing in! Liverpool lead in stoppage time!"

Martin Tyler's match commentary

PREMIER LEAGUE | 3 April 1996

LIVERPOOL 4
Fowler 2, 55
Collymore 68, 90

3 Newcastle United
Ferdinand 10
Ginola 14
Asprilla 57

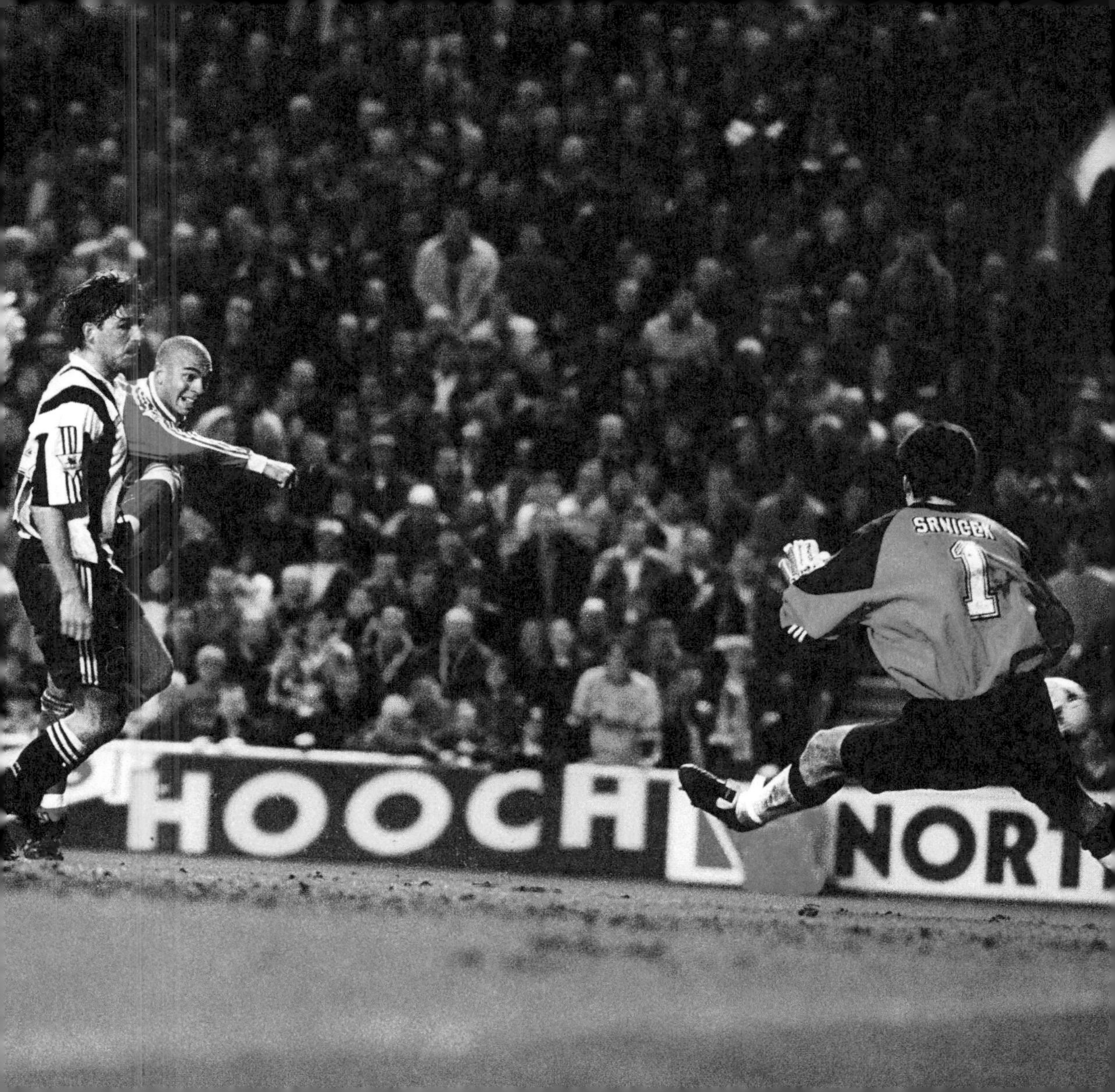
SRNICEK
1
HOOCH
NORT

Steve McMANAMAN

MACCA'S WONDER GOAL

Celtic had struck twice to overturn Michael Owen's early opener and looked set to take a first-leg lead; Steve McManaman decided to take matters into his own hands.

Liverpool didn't have to travel far for their first UEFA Cup fixture of the season, having been drawn with Celtic, located just over 200 miles north of Anfield. Things started well at Celtic Park when Michael Owen scored his first ever European goal, but second-half strikes from Jackie McNamara and Simon Donnelly seemed to have put Celtic in the driving seat as the final whistle approached. But then Steve McManaman intervened. Picking up the ball in the right wing-back position, McManaman used a clever first touch to take himself past his marker, who eventually gave up trying to chase him. Unchallenged, the winger glided inwards for a further 40 yards. As he approached the edge of the box, a swarm of green-and-white hooped shirts attempted to close him down but he calmly pulled the trigger, conjuring up a beautiful curling shot which cracked the inside of the left-hand post and rolled in to save Liverpool.

UEFA CUP | 16 September 1997

Celtic	2	**2**	**LIVERPOOL**
McNamara 53			Owen 6
Donnelly 74			McManaman 89

" This is McManaman, he's got two up with him…McManaman on his own… it's there!"

John Motson's match commentary

Patrik **BERGER**

PASS AND MOVE PERFECTION

Emile Heskey's individual excellence had put Derby County to the sword, but Gérard Houllier's charges showcased the brilliance of the team late on to cap a superb afternoon.

Emile Heskey's first Liverpool hat-trick effectively ended the contest at Pride Park before the 70-minute mark, but there was still enough time left for the visitors to heap more pain on their beaten hosts. And they did it by channelling the club's famed old mantra of 'pass and move'. By the time Patrik Berger set himself to rifle the ball past Mart Poom from 20 yards out in the 81st minute, Liverpool had exchanged 17 passes without interruption over the course of the preceding 48 seconds of play. It all started with Berger himself, who touched the ball back to Christian Ziege on the left-hand touchline. A sequence of careful and measured passes and moments of possession ensued until Danny Murphy rolled the ball toward Nicky Barmby, who dummied it for Berger. The Czech midfielder took one touch to control the ball, and another to tee himself up, before slamming it hard and low into the right-hand corner from outside the box.

Patrik Berger became the first Czech player to play for Liverpool when he made his club debut in September 1996.

" What a goal…Patrik Berger finishes off the move of the season!"

Alan Parry's match commentary

PREMIER LEAGUE | 15 October 2000

Derby County	0	**4 LIVERPOOL**
		Heskey 17, 55, 67
		Berger 81

Robbie **FOWLER**

ONE-TOUCH WONDER

Liverpool had waited five long years to reach a cup final; they ended up needing divine intervention from the man known as 'God' to see off Birmingham City and claim the prize.

The League Cup bore particular significance for Robbie Fowler, Liverpool's No.9. His first six goals in a Liverpool shirt arrived in the competition, while it was also the first trophy he laid his hands on, back in 1995. As the only surviving member of the side that beat Bolton at Wembley six years earlier, it was entirely fitting that he set the ball in motion for the Reds to claim the trophy for the sixth time. Stéphane Henchoz despatched a long, hanging clearance from the back and Emile Heskey rose intelligently to knock it down toward his strike partner. Fowler allowed the ball to bounce once before guiding it, first-time, over and beyond goalkeeper Ian Bennett with consummate ease from 25 yards out. Darren Purse's 90th-minute leveller prevented Fowler from scoring the winning goal, but the striker netted in the ensuing penalty shoot-out to help Liverpool secure the first of the three trophies that they would win that season.

> *" And Fowler produces an absolutely magnificent goal to give the Premiership club the lead."*
>
> **Alan Parry's match commentary**

Fowler scored in the finals of the League Cup and the UEFA Cup in the 2000–01 season

LEAGUE CUP FINAL	25 February 2001	
LIVERPOOL	1 1	Birmingham City
Fowler 30		*Purse 90*
After extra-time Liverpool win 5-4 on penalties		

Gary McALLISTER

THE WHOLE 44 YARDS

**Like a pendulum, the momentum in this typically feisty
Merseyside derby swung from one side to the other. That is,
of course, until Gary McAllister settled it once and for all.**

Having twice taken the lead, through Emile Heskey and Markus Babbel,
Liverpool were pegged back on two occasions, with David Unsworth
taking advantage of Robbie Fowler's missed penalty to make it 2-2
with seven minutes left. Despite being a man down after Igor Biščan's
dismissal, Liverpool refused to shut up shop and accept a solitary point,
and they were awarded a free-kick in the Everton half when Grégory
Vignal was brought down five yards ahead of the centre circle, deep
into stoppage time. Gary McAllister, the coolest head in Goodison Park,
gestured for his team-mates on the far side of the box to move forward
as he stood over the dead ball. But as the mass of blue and red shirts
readied themselves to jostle for a centre in the middle of the box, the
veteran Scot, with the unerring precision of a snooker player potting the
final black, curled the ball into the far left corner of Paul Gerrard's goal to
dramatically claim the local bragging rights for the Liverpool fans.

PREMIER LEAGUE | 16 April 2001

Everton	2	3 LIVERPOOL
Ferguson 42		Heskey 5
Unsworth 83		Babbel 58
		McAllister 90

" Gary had a tremendous game."

Gérard Houllier

Michael **OWEN**

SMASH AND GRAB STRIKE

Throughout history, only a handful of players have had finals unofficially named after them; Michael Owen broke Arsenal hearts to join that elite group.

After dominating the first 70 minutes of the first FA Cup Final to take place outside England, Arsenal went in front through Fredrik Ljungberg, who rounded Sander Westerveld to slot the ball into an empty net. It was no less than they deserved. That breakthrough aroused Liverpool's fighting spirit and after Arsenal's failure to clear a free-kick into their box, Michael Owen showed his characteristic predatory instinct to level it up with seven minutes left on the clock. It was his seventh goal in four games, and he wasn't finished yet. Five minutes later, Patrik Berger lofted a quite magnificent 50-yard ball forward toward the left channel, where his speedy colleague was engaged in a foot race with Lee Dixon. Having surged past the full-back with ease, Owen took one touch to the left, narrowing the angle, before despatching the ball back across goal, with his weaker left foot, into the bottom right-hand corner. Victory had been snatched from the jaws of defeat.

" I never felt the same intense feeling of euphoria scoring any of my other goals as the one that beat David Seaman in Cardiff." **Michael Owen**

Michael Owen became the first British player to win the Ballon d'Or in 22 years when he was handed the prestigious award in 2001.

FA CUP	12 May 2001		
LIVERPOOL	**2**	1	Arsenal
Owen 83, 88			Ljungberg 72

John Arne **RIISE**

RIISE'S ROCKET

Summer signing John Arne Riise had shown his new supporters what he could do with an earlier goal against Everton; he earned a place in their hearts for ever with an unforgettable thunderbolt against the biggest rivals of all.

John Arne Riise scored 31 goals in 348 appearances during his seven-season spell at Liverpool.

The meeting of England's two most successful clubs always inspires unmatched levels of intrigue and excitement on both sides of the M62, and the Premiership match that took place at Anfield in November 2001 was no different. Michael Owen, who notched a brace, proved to be United's scourge, but it was his team-mate John Arne Riise who provoked scenes of delirium in every corner of the famous old stadium. Shortly before half-time, the hosts were awarded a free-kick, six yards outside the box. Dietmar Hamann stood over the ball and nudged it sideways into the path of the Norwegian, who had already commenced his run-up. Riise, unfazed by the fact Quinton Fortune had broken out of the assembled wall and was charging toward him, didn't break stride and ferociously blasted the ball toward the top left-hand corner, where it kissed the crossbar before scraping the back of Fabien Barthez's net at 70mph. It was the picture-book moment of Liverpool's fourth successive win over United.

" It was unbelievable – I've never seen a shot hit so hard and so accurately." **Michael Owen**

PREMIER LEAGUE | 4 November 2001

LIVERPOOL	**3**	1 Manchester United
Owen 31, 51		Beckham 50
Riise 39		

Dietmar **HAMANN**

Dietmar Hamann scored the last ever goal at the old Wembley Stadium when Germany beat England 1-0 in October 2000.

THE KAISER SILENCES POMPEY

Dietmar Hamann didn't score very often during his seven-year stint on Merseyside, but when he did, the goals tended to be very special indeed.

A run of one win in seven had seriously threatened Liverpool's hopes of securing a top-four finish, but Portsmouth's arrival at Anfield in the spring of 2004 provided Gérard Houllier's men with the perfect opportunity to revive their season. And a spectacular early goal from Hamann was just the tonic Liverpool needed to get their mission back on track. After Harry Kewell's flighted corner from the right failed to cause any significant danger, Michael Owen did well to keep the attack alive by drifting over to the left flank. From there he looked up and, having clocked the movement forward of the unmarked Dietmar Hamann, chipped the ball back toward the edge of the 'D'. The German, without breaking stride, connected with the ball perfectly to produce a textbook volley, with the ideal blend of sheer raw power and dexterous swerve. Goalkeeper Shaka Hislop, like the rest of the spectators in attendance at Anfield, could only watch on as the ball threatened to burst the back of the net.

PREMIER LEAGUE | 17 March 2004

LIVERPOOL   **3**   0   Portsmouth
Hamann 6
Owen 28, 58

" It was great to see my volley go into the top corner – it's possibly the best goal I have scored for Liverpool."

Dietmar Hamann

Neil **MELLOR**

MELLOR'S MISSILE

A number of home-grown strikers, such as Robbie Fowler and Michael Owen, have brought Anfield to its feet over the years; now Neil Mellor was about to follow suit.

For Liverpool, who had recorded one win in four league games, the visit of defending champions Arsenal was a daunting one, especially as they hadn't beaten the Londoners in the Premiership for nearly four years. Xabi Alonso's well-worked first-half opener was cancelled out by Patrick Vieira's neat leveller, and the two teams looked set to share the spoils. Fortunately for the majority of the 43,730 spectators packed inside Anfield on a cold November afternoon, Neil Mellor had other ideas. Chris Kirkland drove a long free-kick into the opposition half, and the ball was allowed to bounce toward the box. After Harry Kewell challenged for the ball with Arsenal's centre-backs, it landed, invitingly, in front of Mellor. Twenty-five yards from goal, and with Vieira breathing down his neck, Mellor conjured up a swerving, dipping right-footed volley, which snaked its way into the bottom left-hand corner of the Kop-end goal. The Arsenal hoodoo was over.

Mellor's father, Ian, was a professional footballer who played for a number of clubs, most notably Manchester City.

" For Neil to score his first Premiership goal in front of the Kop was a great moment."

Rafa Benítez

PREMIER LEAGUE | 28 November 2004

LIVERPOOL	**2**	1	Arsenal
Alonso 41			*Vieira 57*
Mellor 90			

Steven **GERRARD**

"OH YOU BEAUTY!"

Liverpool were four minutes away from seeing their Champions League dream die; their heroic captain was not about to let that happen.

Substitutes Florent Sinama-Pongolle and Neil Mellor had overturned Rivaldo's opener in the second half, but the mission remained the same for Liverpool: beat Olympiakos by two goals to avoid Champions League elimination. As the clock wore on, the pressure increased and the hope started to fade. But then Steven Gerrard, in characteristic fashion, decided to grab the game by the scruff of the neck. Mellor got his head to a chip forward and knocked the ball down into his captain's path. The midfielder, who was outside the box, left of centre, carefully approached the ball as Anastasios Pantos tried to close him down. But before the defender could reach him, Gerrard struck across the ball with the right side of his right foot. The thunderous power and missile-like precision of the strike sent it past goalkeeper Antonis Nikopolidis in a flash. Gerrard with arms aloft and fists clenched, set off toward the Kop, safe in the knowledge that Liverpool would not be waking up in the UEFA Cup.

Steven Gerrard has scored more goals in Europe for Liverpool than any other player in the club's history.

"Ohhhhh…you beauty!
What a hit son, what a hit!"

Andy Gray's match commentary

CHAMPIONS LEAGUE	8 December 2004		
LIVERPOOL	**3**	1	Olympiakos
Sinama-Pongolle 47			*Rivaldo 80*
Mellor 80			
Gerrard 86			

Luis GARCIA

Luis Garcia scored in all three knockout rounds of Liverpool's triumphant Champions League campaign in 2005 before they reached the final.

LITTLE MAGICIAN CASTS HIS SPELL

Juventus had conceded just one goal in their previous eight Champions League fixtures when they turned up at Anfield; Liverpool exposed their vulnerability inside the space of 25 blistering minutes.

Juventus, who had one of the most fêted managers of his generation, Fabio Capello, on the bench, a galaxy of established European stars in the squad and a water-tight defence, it certainly looked as though they would provide a tough test for Liverpool in the Champions League. But buoyed on by a boisterous Anfield, the Reds upset the odds to take the lead after 10 minutes through Sami Hyypia's first-time volley. And then, 15 minutes later, things got even better. Anthony Le Tallec, who was on the right-hand side, flicked the ball into the path of the advancing Luis Garcia. The ball sat up perfectly for the Spaniard, who struck a smooth dipping half-volley with his left foot from fully 25 yards, which veered from the centre to the left-hand side of the net behind the flailing Gianluigi Buffon. Fabio Cannavaro pulled one back in the second half, but Liverpool kept a clean sheet in Turin in the second leg to advance to the last four.

CHAMPIONS LEAGUE | 5 April 2005

LIVERPOOL	**2**	1	Juventus
Hyypia 10			*Cannavaro 63*
Garcia 25			

" Le Tallec to Luis Garcia, tries his luck…oh, what a goal!"

Clive Tyldesley's match commentary

Steven GERRARD

COMETH THE HOUR, COMETH THE MAN

Liverpool were 3-0 down at half-time in Europe's showpiece match; they needed a miracle. One man was about to deliver it.

As the massed ranks of Milan's defence back-pedalled, Xabi Alonso picked out John Arne Riise on the left. His first attempt at a cross was charged down by Cafu, jockeying five feet away. The ball went straight back to Riise who had time to steady himself, look up and measure a pin-point centre. Simultaneously Steven Gerrard ghosted in from the edge of the area towards the penalty spot. Jaap Stam realised the danger too late and remained rooted to the floor, team-mates Alessandro Nesta and Paolo Maldini preoccupied with marking duties. Gerrard rose unchallenged, his neck muscles flexed to power the ball past a stranded Dida. It was Liverpool's first headed goal of the tournament. More significantly, it was Milan 3 Liverpool 1; six minutes later it was 3-3.

Steven Gerrard's goal laid the foundation for Liverpool to win the European Cup for the fifth time.

" In towards Gerrard …
Captain's goal! …
Here we go!"

Clive Tyldesley's match commentary

CHAMPIONS LEAGUE FINAL	25 May 2005		
AC Milan	3	**3**	**LIVERPOOL**
Maldini 1			*Gerrard 54*
Crespo 39, 44			*Smicer 56*
			Alonso 59
After extra-time; Liverpool won 3-2 on penalties			

Steven **GERRARD**

CAPTAIN FANTASTIC SAVES THE DAY

Steven Gerrard lit up the Millennium Stadium, providing a sumptuous assist for Djibril Cissé before making it 2–2 with an angled finish from inside the box, but he saved his best for when Liverpool needed it the most.

Steven Gerrard has scored in the finals of the FA Cup, the League Cup, the UEFA Cup and the Champions League.

As the stadium announcer indicated four minutes of stoppage time in the FA Cup Final, Liverpool trailed West Ham 3-2 and faced the very real prospect of going back to Merseyside empty-handed. Step forward, Steven Gerrard. John Arne Riise lofted the ball from the left, more in hope than expectation, toward Fernando Morientes in the box but Danny Gabbidon batted it away with his head, seemingly clearing the danger. The ball bounced twice, and skipped over Djibril Cissé's foot, before dropping in front of Gerrard 35 yards out. The captain, his weary legs afflicted by cramp, swung his right foot with all of his might and caught the ball perfectly on the half-volley. Like an arrow, the ball cut through the crowd of bodies and whizzed into the bottom left-hand corner, well beyond Shaka Hislop's grasp. For the second year in a row Liverpool went on to win on penalties, but Gerrard's iconic contribution defined their triumph.

" I couldn't believe how far out he was when he hit his second goal."

Kenny Dalglish

FA CUP FINAL | 13 May 2006

LIVERPOOL	**3**	3 West Ham United

After extra-time: Liverpool won 3-1 penalties

Cissé 32	*Carragher OG 2*
Gerrard 54, 90	*Ashton 28*
	Konchesky 64

Steven Gerrard prepares to land after launching a simply magnificent 35-yard half-volley toward the bottom left-hand corner of the goal in the last minute of the 2006 FA Cup Final.

Daniel **AGGER**

GREAT DANE'S STRIKE

The Kop was celebrating its 100th birthday and Daniel Agger turned up to the party with the perfect present after West Ham United had taken an early lead.

Three and a half months after contesting one of the most entertaining cup finals in the modern era, Liverpool and West Ham locked horns once again on a bright late-summer afternoon at Anfield. Points, not silverware, were at stake this time, and the visitors took the initiative through Bobby Zamora. Liverpool's response came from an unlikely source, with Daniel Agger, who had been without a goal since moving to Anfield seven months earlier, opening his account in magnificent fashion shortly before the interval. Having received the ball from Xabi Alonso just inside the centre circle, Agger strode forward confidently in a manner reminiscent of Anfield legend Alan Hansen. As the visiting defenders backed off, the Danish centre-back unleashed a vicious left-footed drive from fully 35 yards which flew past the helpless Roy Carroll in the West Ham goal.

" I promise you I was not surprised to see Agger score this fantastic goal because he has a great shot on him and he does that in training."

Rafa Benitez

Daniel Agger, who has got the initials of 'You'll Never Walk Alone' tattooed on the knuckles of his right hand, is a qualified tattoo artist.

PREMIER LEAGUE | 26 August 2006

LIVERPOOL	2	1	West Ham United
Agger 42			*Zamora 12*
Crouch 45			

Xabi **ALONSO**

LIGHTNING STRIKES TWICE FOR ALONSO

Xabi Alonso had showcased his ability from distance with a goal from inside his own half against Luton Town during the previous winter – surely the silky Spaniard couldn't manage the impressive feat again?

Newcastle's visits to Anfield in the Premier League era have produced a catalogue of memorable moments, but few will forget what transpired when the North East side travelled to Merseyside in September 2006. Not least Xabi Alonso. Having played a key role in Dirk Kuyt's opener, Alonso took it upon himself to safeguard all three points as the match entered the closing stages. After dispossessing Charles N'Zogbia midway inside his own half, the midfielder glanced to the right and weighed up his options. Referee Mark Halsey's positioning prevented the Spaniard from switching the play and as he approached the edge of the centre circle, roughly 70 yards from the opposition goal, he opted to shoot. Instead of lifting the ball, Alonso drilled it high and hard. Newcastle goalkeeper Steve Harper scuttled back in desperation toward his line but slipped, powerless to prevent the ball from hitting the back of the net. Alonso turned round and threw himself into Pepe Reina's arms in celebration.

PREMIER LEAGUE | 20 September 2006

LIVERPOOL   **2**   0   Newcastle United
Kuyt 29
Alonso 79

" ...their keeper was well out of the goal, so I gave it a try."
Xabi Alonso

Peter **CROUCH**

CROUCH'S SENSATIONAL SCISSOR-KICK

Anfield has played host to many magical moments on those famous European nights; Peter Crouch wrote his name into continental folklore when he stunned Galatasaray with a strike sweeter than Turkish Delight.

Crouch's acrobatic strike against Galatasaray was voted one of the top ten goals in UEFA's history.

After a 0-0 draw at PSV Eindhoven in their opening Champions League group-stage fixture, Liverpool needed a strong showing at home to Turkish giants Galatasaray on matchday two. Early goals from Peter Crouch and Luis García settled the nerves and handed Liverpool the advantage, but it was the former's second strike which ultimately proved to be the winner and secured the England striker's place in Anfield folklore. Steve Finnan got the better of Orhan Ak on the right flank and whipped in an inviting ball slightly behind Crouch, who was waiting on the penalty spot. Although the forward was unmarked, he opted against controlling the ball and steadying himself. Instead, he lifted all 200cm (6'7") of his body off the ground and, like a contortionist, despatched a thunderous first-time scissor-kick into the bottom right-hand corner, leaving goalkeeper Faryd Mondragón rooted to the spot.

> " *Crouch scored an amazing goal and he showed very good movement and how good a player he is.*"
>
> *Rafa Benitez*

CHAMPIONS LEAGUE	27 September 2006	
LIVERPOOL	**3**	2 Galatasaray
Crouch 9, 52		Ümit 59, 65
Garcia 14		

Fernando **TORRES**

TORRES STORMS OLD TRAFFORD

Nearly five years had passed since Liverpool had beaten their fiercest rivals at Old Trafford, but all that was about to change, even though Ronaldo had put United in front from the penalty spot.

Martin Skrtel hoofed the ball upfield into the United half and Nemanja Vidic curiously opted to let the ball bounce. Like a voracious fox bearing down on a hapless rabbit, Torres seized on the Serbian's indecision, leaping with his right foot forward to nick the ball and leave the defender in his wake on the turf. As Torres eased his way toward Edwin van der Sar, the goalkeeper stood tall as he tried to outwit the Spaniard but it was to no avail, as the striker unerringly guided the ball inside the left-hand post to level the score. The stunned home crowd were treated to a five-finger gesture from the Spaniard – a nod to the quintet of European Cups that can be found in the Anfield trophy room – and things got even worse for United later on as further strikes from Steven Gerrard, Fábio Aurélio and Andrea Dossena consigned them to their heaviest home defeat in 17 years and propelled Liverpool back into the title race.

PREMIER LEAGUE | 14 March 2009

Manchester United	1	**4 LIVERPOOL**
Ronaldo 23		Torres 28
		Gerrard 44
		Aurelio 77
		Dossena 90

" We knew that maybe with Fernando's movement we could create problems for the defenders."

Rafa Benítez

Fernando **TORRES**

EL NIÑO GIVES CHELSEA THE BLUES

The champions arrived on Merseyside boasting the meanest defence in the league; Liverpool's number nine was about to shatter their sheen of invincibility with two flashes of his trusty right foot.

The sight of Chelsea's blue shirts seemed to bring out the very best in Fernando Torres and the visit of Carlo Ancelotti's league leaders on a cold November afternoon prompted more of the same. Having made the most of a superb lofted pass from Dirk Kuyt to break the deadlock early on, the Spaniard, who had won the World Cup four months earlier, sealed a morale-boosting win with a touch of genius moments before the interval. Stationed just outside the box on the left wing, Torres received a sharp pass from Raul Meireles. Now courting the attention of Branislav Ivanovic, the striker forced the defender to retreat back into his area and, as the smallest of gaps emerged, opened up his right foot and bent the ball past the Serbian and beyond Cech into the far corner of the net, prompting pandemonium in the stands.

Torres reached 50 goals for Liverpool in just 84 appearances, faster than any other player in the club's history.

" He finished his goals in a brilliant way – he is getting better and better."

Dirk Kuyt

PREMIER LEAGUE | 7 November 2010

LIVERPOOL   **2**   0   Chelsea
Torres 11, 44

Luis **SUÁREZ**

HALFWAY LINE SHOT SEALS HAT-TRICK

Suárez had already terrorised Norwich with two quick-fire goals in the first half, and he left an indelible mark in East Anglia with a simply breathtaking third.

Norwich skipper Elliott Ward had been run ragged by a particularly effervescent Luis Suárez over the course of the preceding 82 minutes, but even he could not have expected what would follow when the striker dispossessed him on the halfway line after he had trapped a long ball forward from Glen Johnson. Spotting goalkeeper John Ruddy 12 yards off his line, Suárez ignored the call from captain Steven Gerrard, who was approaching on his left, and spectacularly launched the ball high into the East Anglian evening sky, watching its descent carefully as it completed its mesmerising 50-yard journey and caressed the back of the net before landing on the sodden Carrow Road turf. Suárez wheeled away in celebration toward the away supporters, who had just witnessed a spectacular conclusion to the Uruguayan's first hat-trick as a Liverpool player.

Norwich were Suárez's most frequent victims during his spell at Anfield – he netted 12 times against the East Anglia club.

" It was on the tip of my tongue to give him a rollocking, but then he did that – it was great finishing."

Steven Gerrard

PREMIER LEAGUE | 28 April 2012

Norwich City   0   **3 LIVERPOOL**

Suárez 24, 28, 82

A beaming Luis Suárez leaps with delight after capping his maiden Liverpool hat-trick in style with an audacious long-range strike against Norwich City in April 2012.

Luis **SUÁREZ**

THREE STEPS TO KOP HEAVEN

Liverpool have a rich tradition of goalscoring legends; Uruguayan international striker Luis Suàrez was about to join the pantheon with this sublimely taken goal against Newcastle United.

When José Enrique launched a sixty-yard high ball from close to the left touchline, it looked distinctly speculative, hopeful at best. The Spanish defender, however, evidently knew the outrageous ability of its intended target, the mercurial Uruguayan Luis Suàrez, then in hot goalscoring form. Three touches later it rested in the back of the Newcastle net. As the defence-bypassing missile flew over Steven Taylor's head, Suarez stole half a yard on Fabricio Coloccini as they approached the penalty area. Suàrez, at full gallop, controlled the dropping ball on the Liverpool crest on his chest, taking it further away from the flagging Coloccini. The second touch sidestepped the onrushing Tim Krul in the manner of an expert matador, the third applied the coup de grace into an empty net. The Kop erupted.

" His first touch coming from that height was an incredible piece of skill."

Brendan Rodgers

PREMIER LEAGUE | 4 November 2012

LIVERPOOL   **1**   1 Newcastle United
Suárez 67   *Cabaye 43*

Philippe **COUTINHO**

SAMBA STYLE ARRIVES AT ANFIELD

As the Anfield faithful waved goodbye to one hero, Jamie Carragher, they welcomed the birth of another – Philippe Coutinho.

As Philippe Coutinho prepared to receive the ball from Jordon Ibe 30 yards from goal, there appeared to be little on for the diminutive Brazilian maestro. There were five blue-and-white hooped shirts in front of him while Shaun Derry, who had unsuccessfully tried to dispossess Ibe moments earlier, was now set on closing him down. Taking one touch to control the ball and set himself, Coutinho pulled back his right leg and subsequently unleashed a fizzing low drive, with just a touch of swerve, which briefly hovered above the pristine turf before unerringly finding its way into the bottom right-hand corner of Rob Green's goal at the Anfield Road end. It proved to be the only goal of the game and it ensured a perfect send-off for Jamie Carragher, who was making his final appearance in a red shirt.

Philipe Coutinho is one of only five Brazilian players who have played for Liverpool in the club's history.

" He's been a real find for us in terms of the price we paid."

Brendan Rodgers

PREMIER LEAGUE	19 May 2013		
LIVERPOOL	**1**	0	Queens Park Rangers
Coutinho 23			

Daniel **STURRIDGE**

STURRIDGE'S SUMPTUOUS CHIP

Luis Suárez had enthralled Anfield with a clinical treble, but it was his strike partner Daniel Sturridge who left the home supporters open-mouthed in awe.

With just over 13 minutes left on the clock, West Brom midfielder Youssouf Mulumbu jostled for a loose ball with Steven Gerrard before accidentally nodding into the path of the lurking Daniel Sturridge. The striker trapped the ball and, with Mulumbu in pursuit, glided from the centre of the park toward the left-hand side of the area, with the opposition defenders frantically back-pedalling. As he approached the edge of the area at full pace, and with goalkeeper Ben Foster little more than four yards off his line, Sturridge, in the blink of an eye, somehow conjured up enough backlift to get the ball out of his feet. The weight, the finesse and the trajectory were perfect, as the ball evaded Foster's outstretched glove before dropping just inside the top right-hand corner. By the time Foster was back on his feet, Sturridge was already 'riding the wave' in celebration.

Daniel Sturridge is one of only two players in Premier League history who have scored in eight successive Premier League matches.

" I think Daniel scored the best goal to be honest."

Lucas Leiva

PREMIER LEAGUE | 26 October 2013

LIVERPOOL	**4**	1	West Bromwich Albion
Suárez 12, 17, 55			*Morrison 66*
Sturridge 77			

INDEX

CREDITS

Captain Steven Gerrard makes a beeline toward the Kop after thumping the ball past Olympiakos goalkeeper Antonis Nikopolidis to keep Liverpool in the Champions League in December 2004.

The publishers would like to thank the following sources for their kind permission to reproduce the pictures in this book.

Imagery © Liverpool Football Club & Athletic Grounds Ltd. with the following exceptions:
Action Images: 74-75; /Frank Baron/Sporting Pictures: 60; /Eddie Keogh/Reuters: 101; Tony
Marshall/Sporting Pictures: 59; /Darren Staples/Reuters: 107; /Darren Walsh: 72
Colorsport: 20; /Andrew Cowie: 4-5, 25, 29, 63; /Stewart Fraser: 36
Getty Images: /Allsport: 67; /Shaun Botterill: 91; /Clive Brunskill: 86; /Simon Bruty: 65; /Stu Forster: 79; /Laurence Griffiths: 92, 108;
/Alex Livesey: 111; /Manchester Daily Express: 51; Popperfoto: 23; /Ben Radford: 77, 85; /Bob Thomas: 33, 54, 68; /Andrew Yates/
AFP: 112
Press Association Images: 26; /Stephen Pond: 117; /Nick Potts: 83
Rex Features: /Associated Newspapers: 57; /Ted Blackbrow/Daily Mail: 71